PLANETARY
EXPLORATION

# EARTH

## JASON CARTER

**Britannica®**
Educational Publishing

IN ASSOCIATION WITH

**ROSEN**
EDUCATIONAL SERVICES

Published in 2017 by Britannica Educational Publishing (a trademark of Encyclopædia Britannica, Inc.) in association with The Rosen Publishing Group, Inc.
29 East 21st Street, New York, NY 10010

Distributed exclusively by Rosen Publishing.
To see additional Britannica Educational Publishing titles, go to rosenpublishing.com.


First Edition

**Britannica Educational Publishing**
J.E. Luebering: Executive Director, Core Editorial
Mary Rose McCudden: Editor, Britannica Student Encyclopedia

**Rosen Publishing**
Nicholas Croce: Editor
Nelson Sá: Art Director
Michael Moy: Designer
Cindy Reiman: Photography Manager
Karen Huang: Photo Researcher

**Library of Congress Cataloging-in-Publication Data**

Names: Carter, Jason (Children's author)
Title: Earth / Jason Carter.
Description: New York : Britannica Educational Publishing in association with Rosen Educational Services, 2017. | Series: Planetary exploration | Includes bibliographical references and index.
Identifiers: LCCN 2016020467 | ISBN 9781508104117 (library bound) | ISBN 9781508104124 (pbk.) | ISBN 9781508103059 (6-pack)
Subjects: LCSH: Earth (Planet)—Juvenile literature. | Solar system—Juvenile literature.
Classification: LCC QB631.4 .C3786 2017 | DDC 525—dc23
LC record available at https://lccn.loc.gov/2016020467


*Manufactured in China*

# CONTENTS

# A SPECIAL PLACE

Earth is the third planet from the sun and one of eight planets in our solar system. Earth orbits, or travels around, the sun at an average distance of about 93 million miles (150 kilometers). Earth appears bright blue and white when viewed from outer space.

Earth is a special planet. It is the only planet in the universe known to support life. Life is possible on Earth thanks to the oxygen in its air and water on its surface.

**A satellite flying 435 miles (700 km) over Earth captured this beautiful image of our unique planet.**

## THINK ABOUT IT

**Earth's average temperature can change. How might rising average temperatures affect humans?**

Earth's atmosphere also is the perfect temperature for life, averaging about 59° F (15° C). It is not too hot, like Venus, or too cold, like Neptune. But Earth is always changing due to its many cycles and systems. Understanding how these cycles and systems work is important because human activities continue to affect the planet's surface, oceans, and atmosphere.

**A photograph taken at night shows the lights of the populated areas of Taiwan and mainland China.**

# EARTH'S AMAZING FEATURES

**E**arth is the fifth largest planet in the solar system. Scientists have figured out that Earth's mass is about 5,972,000,000,000,000,000,000,000 tons!

Land covers about 30 percent of Earth's surface. Seven large continents make up Earth's landmass. They are Africa, Antarctica, Asia, Australia, Europe, North America, and South America. Asia is the largest continent and Australia is the smallest.

Water covers about 70 percent of the planet's surface. The

**This sheet of ice and snow is known as a glacier. Most of Earth's surface is covered with water or ice.**

four major water bodies on Earth are the Arctic, Atlantic, Pacific, and Indian oceans. They surround the continents. Some of the water on Earth is frozen. For example, there are large ice sheets in the Arctic and Antarctic regions.

The layer of gases surrounding Earth is the atmosphere. This is the air that living things need to breathe. Earth's atmosphere reaches up to several hundred miles above the surface. Other planets also have atmospheres. Unlike Earth, though, most other planets' atmospheres cannot support life.

**These Alaskan mountains are part of the landmass that makes up the North American continent.**

# INSIDE EARTH

Crust

Upper
Mantle

Mantle

Core

Inner
Core

**Earth's structure is made up of
three main layers: the core, the
mantle, and the crust.**

Three main layers make up planet Earth: the core, mantle, and crust. The core is the very center of the planet. It is about 4,300 miles (6,900 kilometers) thick. The temperature gets hotter in Earth's deeper layers. The temperature in the core is about 10,000 degrees Fahrenheit (6,000° C). That's as hot as the surface of the sun!

The mantle covers the core. It is about 1,800 miles (2,900 kilometers) thick. The temperature at

**Compare Earth's mantle and its crust. In what ways are they different?**

the bottom of the mantle is about 6,700 degrees Fahrenheit (3,700° C).

The crust is Earth's thin, rocky outer layer. Plants, animals, and people live on the crust. At its thickest, the crust is about 19 miles (31 kilometers) deep. No one has ever dug all the way through Earth's crust. The deepest well ever drilled, on the Kola Peninsula in Russia, is about 7.62 miles (12.26 kilometers) deep.

Volcanic eruptions take place when hot gases and melted rock rush up from the mantle and blast through Earth's crust.

# A ROCKY PLACE

Earth is made mostly of rock. All rocks are made of smaller substances called minerals. Some minerals are metals, such as gold, silver, copper, and platinum. Other minerals, such as diamonds and salt, are crystals.

There are three main kinds of rock: igneous, metamorphic, and sedimentary. Igneous rock is formed when magma cools and hardens. Magma is hot, melted rock from deep in the mantle. The most common igneous rock in Earth's crust is granite.

Metamorphic rocks are formed when other rocks are affected by

**Quartz is one of the most common minerals on Earth. It is found in most types of rock, including granite, sandstone, and marble.**

great temperatures and pressures. Examples of metamorphic rocks include marble and slate.

Sedimentary rocks form at or near Earth's surface. They are made when small particles of other worn-down rocks form layers and are squeezed together over time. Sedimentary rocks cover most of the surface of Earth but are often covered by soil. Sandstone and limestone are examples of sedimentary rock.

Yosemite National Park is known for its very high cliffs. The igneous rock known as granite makes up most of Yosemite's cliff formations.

# THE ROCK CYCLE

Nothing on planet Earth stays the same—not even rocks! Even the hardest rocks are constantly being broken down into minerals by different forces. Then the minerals from old rocks form into new rocks. This process of change that rocks go through is called the rock cycle. Earth has been recycling rocks this way for billions of years.

Weather, heat, and pressure are important to the rock cycle. On Earth's surface, rain, wind, and other weather elements break down igneous rock. The rock breaks into tiny pieces called

**Sedimentary rock is created when layers and layers of mud and sand begin to pile up.**

sediment. Sand and mud are examples of sediment. As sediment builds up in layers, pressure causes new sedimentary rocks to form.

Sometimes many layers of rock form on top of each other. Pressure slowly pushes them down into the Earth. Sometimes, very high pressure will change sedimentary rock into metamorphic rock.

At times sedimentary rock will reach the mantle, where it melts into magma. As magma rises to the surface, it cools and forms new igneous rocks. And the rock cycle continues!

When pressed down into the mantle, sandstone and other rocks melt into magma. Magma that reaches Earth's surface is called lava.

# A BLANKET OF AIR

Compared to that of other planets, such as Mars or Venus, Earth's atmosphere is rich in oxygen. It is made up mostly of nitrogen (71 percent) and oxygen (21 percent). It is also made up of smaller amounts of many other gases, including **carbon dioxide** and water vapor.

The atmosphere has several layers, including the troposphere and the stratosphere. The troposphere is the lowest part of the atmosphere. It extends about 6 miles (10 kilometers) above Earth's surface.

Temperatures decrease as you get higher into the troposphere. Temperatures at the top of the troposphere can be about -70 degrees Fahrenheit (-57° C). Almost

**This image, taken from outer space, shows Earth's atmosphere.**

all Earth's weather, including rain and snow, occurs in the troposphere.

The stratosphere extends to about 30 miles (50 kilometers) above Earth's surface. Temperatures are actually warmer in the stratosphere than in the troposphere. This is because of a substance called ozone. Most of the ozone layer lies within the stratosphere. It is important to life because it absorbs most of the sun's harmful rays.

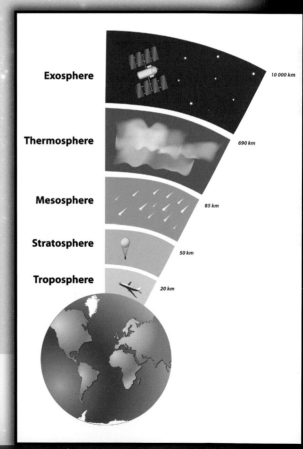

Exosphere — 10 000 km

Thermosphere — 690 km

Mesosphere — 85 km

Stratosphere — 50 km

Troposphere — 20 km

**Earth's atmosphere is made up of many different layers, including the troposphere and the stratosphere.**

# WATER EVERYWHERE

Earth's hydrosphere is made up of all the water on the planet. This includes oceans, lakes, rivers, ice, precipitation, and water vapor. Saltwater oceans and seas make up about 97 percent of the hydrosphere. That means that only about 3 percent of the water on Earth is fresh water. Since humans and animals need fresh water to survive, it is a very important resource.

The average depth of the oceans is about 2.3 miles (3.8 kilo-

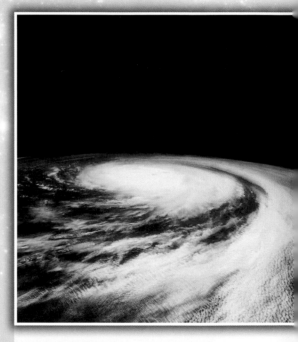

**Earth's surface is mostly water, as seen in this satellite image of a hurricane over the Pacific Ocean.**

meters). The deepest part of the ocean is called the Mariana Trench. It is about 6.86 miles (11.03 kilometers) deep.

When the sun heats ocean water, the water evaporates. This means that the water turns into a gas called water vapor that floats into the air. The water vapor forms clouds. Wind pushes these clouds over land. Then the water vapor condenses and becomes rain or snow. Some of the rain falls into rivers and flows back to the oceans. This is known as the water cycle.

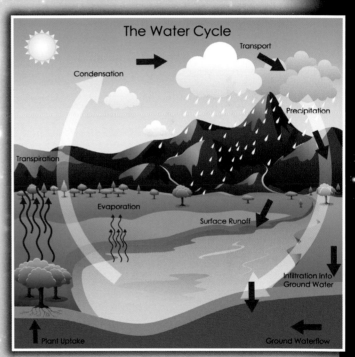

**Water in Earth's hydrosphere cycles from oceans and lakes to the atmosphere and back again.**

# A PLANET FIT FOR LIFE

The biosphere is where life happens. It includes Earth's surface, as well as the hydrosphere and the atmosphere. Most animals live on Earth's surface or in the oceans. However, bats, birds, and some insects live in the atmosphere, too.

Tiny organisms, such as bacteria, also make up the biosphere. Bacteria are one of the most common life forms on Earth. They can live just about anywhere, including high in the atmosphere. Bacteria have even been found living in rock more than a mile (1.6 kilometers) underground.

**Bacteria are one of the most abundant life forms in the biosphere. This image shows bacteria magnified many times.**

**What are three ways that plants help support life on Earth?**

Plants are another important form of life in the biosphere. Humans and other animals need plants to survive. Many plants, such as lettuce, potatoes, and strawberries, can be eaten. Plants also produce oxygen that we need to breathe. Plants absorb carbon dioxide. This helps regulate Earth's temperature. Without plants, carbon dioxide would build up and make the planet too hot to support life.

**Plants in Earth's biosphere absorb carbon dioxide from the atmosphere. They also release oxygen.**

# ALWAYS IN MOTION

Though you don't feel it, Earth is in constant motion. Like all planets, Earth has two types of motion: orbit and spin. Earth's orbit is the path the planet takes around the sun. It takes 365.25 days for Earth to orbit the sun once. This is equal to one calendar year. The force that keeps Earth orbiting the sun is called gravity.

Earth also rotates, or spins, on its axis. The axis is an imaginary line that runs through

**Earth is constantly traveling around the sun. The length of time that it takes to complete one whole trip is called a year.**

**What is the difference between Earth's orbit and its spin?**

Earth's center from the North Pole to the South Pole. It takes 24 hours to complete one rotation. This is equal to one day.

Before the 1500s, most people believed that Earth was motionless. Then astronomer and mathematician Nicolaus Copernicus said that Earth revolves on its axis and orbits around the sun.

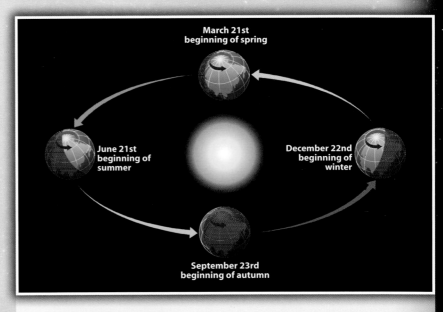

March 21st
beginning of spring

June 21st
beginning of
summer

December 22nd
beginning of
winter

September 23rd
beginning of autumn

**Earth completes one full orbit around the sun every 365.25 days. It also makes one full spin on its axis every day.**

# THE CHANGING SEASONS

**E**arth's axis is tilted in relation to the sun. The North Pole points to the same direction in space as Earth revolves around the sun. Because of this, the northern half of the planet, called the Northern Hemisphere, is tilted toward the sun for about half the year. During this time, the Northern Hemisphere gets more sunlight

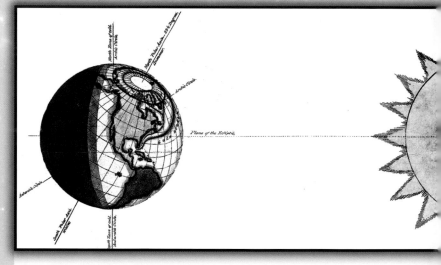

**The part of Earth that is tilted toward the sun will experience spring or summer.**

**How is it possible for it to be winter in North America and summer in South America at the same time?**

than the Southern Hemisphere. During the other half of the year, the Northern Hemisphere is tilted away from the sun. This is when the Southern Hemisphere gets more sun than the Northern Hemisphere.

Earth has seasons because of its fixed, tilted axis. The Northern Hemisphere experiences its warmer seasons when the Southern Hemisphere experiences its colder seasons. The seasons in the two hemispheres are always opposite. As Earth revolves around the sun on its fixed, tilted axis, the seasons change throughout the year.

**Because they need sunlight, flowers bloom during the spring and summer, the seasons that get the most sunlight.**

# AN AMAZING MOON

**A** satellite is a small object that orbits a larger object in space. Earth's moon is one of the largest satellites in the solar system.

The moon is about 239,000 miles (385,000 kilometers) from Earth. The moon's gravity influences Earth. For example, ocean tides are caused by the moon's gravity as it orbits Earth.

The moon's surface is unlike Earth's. The moon is

The moon is Earth's only satellite. It revolves around the planet once every 27 days or so.

**What are some differences between Earth and the moon?**

much dustier, with no water, plants, or any other life forms. However, the moon and Earth do have some things in common. Scientists have discovered rocks from the moon that are made from the same materials as those found in Earth's mantle. Because of this, scientists think that the moon was created out of magma and rock from Earth. This magma and rock may have broken off after a Mars-sized object hit Earth.

**The moon is made from the same rocks and minerals as Earth. The moon was likely once part of Earth.**

# EARTH'S ANCIENT PAST

Earth is approximately 4.6 billion years old. Our planet likely formed from a cloud of gas and dust called a nebula.

Earth's surface has changed a lot since it was first formed. During its earliest period, Earth was covered with red-hot seas of glowing liquid rock. About 250 million years ago, all Earth's land was joined in one large continent called Pangea. Pangea then broke apart into smaller continents. They spread

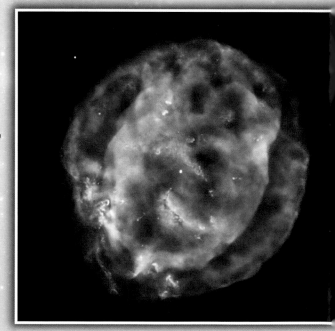

**This large bubble of gas and dust is a nebula. Scientists think that Earth and the rest of our solar system formed from a nebula.**

out by a process called continental drift into all the separate continents we know today.

The surface of Earth changes all the time. Wind, weather, water, volcanoes, and earth-quakes cause these changes. For example, the water in rivers breaks down certain kinds of rock and sometimes forms large canyons. A process called plate tectonics continues to move the continents. Mountain ranges are sometimes formed when differ-ent continental plates smash into one other.

**A drawing shows what Earth might have looked like billions of years ago when it was covered with volcanoes, craters, and lava.**

# THE FUTURE OF OUR PLANET

In the very distant future, Earth will look much different than it does today. Within a few hundred million years, Earth should become so warm that rainforests may grow near the North and South poles. In a billion years, the slowly brightening sun may eventually evaporate all the oceans.

However, many current forms of life on Earth may survive for thousands and even millions of years. This includes human beings.

One current threat to Earth is global warming. Increasing carbon

**The sun grows hotter with age. In a billion years, the sun may evaporate Earth's water.**

**What are some changes humans can make to slow down global warming?**

dioxide levels in the atmosphere causes this warming. It is believed that humans contribute to this problem by burning fossil fuels. If we don't make changes, Earth may continue heating up too quickly. This may cause mass extinctions of other animals and threaten our own long-term survival.

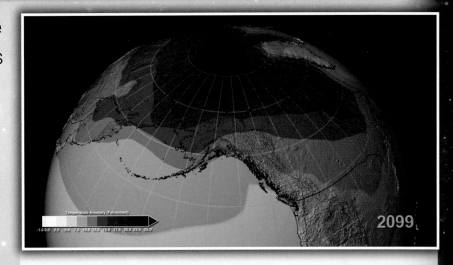

Temperature Anomaly (Fahrenheit)
-1.0 0.0 2.5 5.0 7.5 10.0 12.5 15.0 17.5 20.0 22.5 25.0

2099

**Global climate change is making Earth hotter. Humans may be able to slow down this warming by burning fewer fossil fuels.**

# GLOSSARY

**ATMOSPHERE** The gases that surround Earth, another planet, or a star.

**BACTERIA** A very small single-celled organism that lives in soil, water, or the bodies of plants and animals.

**CONDENSE** To change from a gas to a liquid.

**EXTINCTION** The process of becoming extinct or no longer existing.

**FOSSIL FUEL** Material formed from the remains of organisms that lived long ago. The material produces energy when burned. Petroleum (oil), coal, and natural gas are examples of fossil fuels.

**GRAVITY** A pulling force that works across space. Every object has a force of gravity, but the greater the mass of an object, the greater is its force of gravity.

**HEMISPHERE** One of the halves of Earth as divided by the equator. A hemisphere is a half of any ball-shaped object.

**LANDMASS** A large area of land.

**OXYGEN** A gas that makes up about 21 percent of the air in Earth's atmosphere.

**OZONE** A form of oxygen that is a bluish, sharp-smelling gas containing three atoms per molecule.

**PRECIPITATION** Water or the amount of water that falls to Earth as hail, mist, rain, sleet, or snow.

**RECYCLE** To process and reuse materials such as bottles, cans, and paper waste.

**RESOURCE** A usable stock or supply.

**TIDE** The regular upward and downward movement of the level of the ocean. Tides are caused by the gravitational pull of the sun and the moon on Earth.

**VOLCANO** A vent in Earth's crust from which melted or hot rock and steam come out.

**WATER VAPOR** Water in a gaseous form.

# FOR MORE INFORMATION

## Books

Green, Dan. *Rocks and Minerals*. New York, NY: Scholastic, 2013

Hunter, Nick. *Earth*. Chicago, IL: Raintree, 2013

Oxlade, Chris. *Global Warming*. Mankato, MN: Smart Apple Media, 2012.

Peters, Elisa. *Earth*. New York, NY: PowerKids Press, 2013

Sneideman, Joshua. *Climate Change*. White River Junction, VT: Nomad Press, 2015.

## Websites

Because of the changing nature of internet links, Rosen Publishing has developed an online list of websites related to the subject of this book. This site is updated regularly. Please use this link to access this list:

http://www.rosenlinks.com/pe/earth

# INDEX

DEC     2017